THE
SEARCH
— FOR —
PURPOSE

DISCOVER THE THREE E'S TO FIND YOUR PURPOSE WITH EASE

LOVE, BOBBIE JO

Love, Bobbie Jo/All About Healing, LLC
Kewaunee, WI
LoveBobbieJo.com

The Search for Purpose/ Love, Bobbie Jo. —1st ed.
ISBN 978-1-7361210-2-3

May this book guide you to know and to embody your true purpose.
Love, Bobbie Jo

TABLE OF CONTENTS

FOREWARD

*I*ve spent a lot of time searching for my purpose. Feeling a void for so long that "something" was missing in not knowing what it was. Flailing along in life seeking some greater meaning, something more I was here to do, that somehow eluded me.

A persistent empty feeling, a lost wandering, that all the courses and books and jobs and certifications and roles and you name it—couldn't seem to fill.

Not everyone around me understood what this quest was about, often leaving them frustrated with my seeming lack of happiness and fulfillment (with no apparent external reason for), and I wondered, "How could anyone *not* be on the quest for purpose? After all, isn't that why we are here?"

Then, finally, I realized I was looking in all the wrong places and for the wrong thing.

In this book, I share with you my discovery, with the hope it may bring you that enlightened "aha" that it brought me. That it may lighten your burden in the search. That it may guide you to the very thing you seek.

I invite you to stay curious, grab your favorite writing tool, and open up to uncovering the purpose that is seeking you!

Love, Bobbie Jo

CHAPTER

There is nothing to seek, nothing to find, it has been in you all the time.

WHAT IS PURPOSE?

Simply Love, Simply You.

*B*efore we dive in, let's discuss what we are searching for. What exactly is this purpose that we seek?

If you look at the definition of purpose, it is the reason for something or the meaning of something.

Therefore, when we ponder what our purpose is, we are desiring to know our reason for being—the meaning behind our existence.

That is a big question, especially when we place so much value on knowing the answer in order to create a meaningful existence and to feel fulfilled.

What is the one significant reason why you are here?

I wanted the drive-through version. I wanted to pull my car up, roll down the window and say, "I'll take an order of purpose... with a side of passion, please."

That's how frustrated I was. After all these years, and all this seeking, how could I not have found it yet? Was I the only person on this planet who somehow wasn't given a purpose?

I wanted someone to tell me what the answer was, so I could get on living it already. Time was flying by, and I still didn't know what I was here to do.

What am I meant to do? That question implied that there was something more I needed to achieve, acquire or prove... And I had no idea what it was.

Moments I felt, "Alas, I've found it!" became short-lived as life would remove those purposes through time, change, dissatisfaction or loss.

Even the times my work felt rewarding, deeper within I knew there had to be something more.

I earned more certifications. I tried different jobs. I read more books. I invested in more courses. Nothing seemed to fill the void; my purpose still eluded me.

Finally, I surrendered. I meditated and prayed, pleading for the answer. "God... Who am I? Why am I here? What is my purpose? What is my gift?"

Immediately, clearly and matter-of-factly, I heard, "Love."

I felt my soul exhale, as a wave of knowing and understanding washed over me.

And while a deep part of me could feel this truth, my head was completely perplexed by the simplicity of the answer. I questioned God, "What?! My purpose is love? But God, is that enough? Is that *enough*?"

God's reply, "My child, it is all there is."

It is all there is!

Pause here for a moment... and allow that deep truth to sink in.

Love—is—all—there—is.

In that sacred moment, I finally realized my purpose is not in my *do*-ing, it is in my *be*-ing. It is who I *am.*

It is not something I need to achieve or acquire; it simply is.

It didn't reside somewhere out there to be found. It was always within me.

This opens us up to the foundation of purpose, its truest form, who we are, our divine essence of love.

You cannot know your purpose if you are not aware of your spirit, for that is where it resides. That is where you reside. Purpose is the love and the light that you *are*.

So if your purpose really is this simple, that it is you and your essence, the love that you are, what exactly are you searching for then?

The *experience* of purpose. The experience of *you*. Life offers the opportunity for self-discovery. This human "experience" offers you the ability to know the love that you are, and to express and share that love. It gives you the space to feel and understand contrasts, emotions, sensations, and the ability to create, evolve and grow.

It is from your core purpose—your inner *essence*, the love and the light that you are—that you get to experience and expand your purpose outward into the world.

The reason my purpose eluded me was because I, like most, was searching within the outer expression of purpose. It wasn't until I connected to my essence, my core purpose, that the rest was revealed—the three E's to connect to and experience purpose in life.

In the following chapters, I will dive into each E with exercises to help you connect with and experience your purpose.

THE THREE E'S

Embody

You are a spiritual being having a human experience. You are a soul in a physical body. To live aligned in your purpose, the first step is to embody your essence. Embodying is to become aware of, connect with and feel the divinity of your being within your human being.

Express

Expression is often where we seek to find our purpose—in our doing/our actions. This is where you get to express your essence, the love that you are, in the ways that call to your soul—the ways in which you are guided.

Engage

This is where you get to make your impact, by sharing your embodied essence with the world through its sacred expressions. Here, you experience a feeling of purpose by sharing the love that you are, in the ways you are inspired, to serve and inspire others.

Each of these layers is essential to your purpose. The important part is to start at the inner core they expand upon—*you*.

WHAT I'VE LEARNED:

We often seem to think that what we are missing is out there somewhere, so we go searching outside ourselves, especially when the question that begins the quest—What are you here to *do*?—points us in that direction. When everything we find or try isn't the answer we're looking for, it can feel frustrating. It's about looking inward. What we seek, we already have... It is within us. Ironically, it's often the last place we look.

Your Turn to Reflect.

On the following lines (or in your journal), take a moment to reflect on your quest for purpose. Where have you been seeking it? What have you found on your search? What do you believe purpose truly is?

_____

_____

_____

_____

_____

_____

_____

_____

_____

_____

_____

_____

_____

_____

_____

_____

_____

_____

_____

_____

_____

_____

_____

_____

_____

_____

_____

_____

_____

_____

_____

_____

_____

_____

_____

_____

_____

What is Purpose?

CHAPTER
Two

Breathe in the nature of your soul, it holds all you seek and long to know.

EMBODYING PURPOSE

Being Love.

*E*mbodying your essence—your purpose—is experiencing and feeling the divinity of your being in your earthly physical form. It is in connecting to your soul, so that you express and engage from this sacred alignment.

Embodying is your purpose in *being.*

See, it didn't matter what I *did.* If it wasn't founded in the truth of my essence, who I really am, my wholeness, I would continue to feel a void.

If I didn't know and feel my essence, and know that it alone is enough, that the love that I am is my true purpose, I would continue to try to find, discover, prove, and strive to get it "right" to be enough.

I, like most, was searching for something significant that I must do—that there was something outside of myself that I had to achieve. I was giving my power away to something external.

Whereas the truth is, we are already God's perfection, just as a baby being born is looked upon with loving eyes from its mother. There is no moment of, "Welcome to the world! I can't wait until you prove what you have come here to do." No. That baby is the pureness of divine love come into form. That baby *is* purpose. Ask any mom. And just like that baby, so are you and I.

As we step into this world, and grow, and become shaped by all the things outside us, including the question of, "What are you going to do with your life?," we can lose sight of this essential truth. We can lose conscious awareness of our sacred essence, our enough-ness, as we focus on outside forces.

Think of a dog. What is its purpose? Do you look at him and say, "Fido, what are you going to do with your life?" No. They simply be the love that they are. They express the love that they are. They engage with us as the love that they are. The love that they are is simply enough. They cannot be anything but purpose.

Deeper meaning in life comes when you live from the depths of your soul. When you start by embodying your essence, the truth of who you are, your forms of expressing and engaging become fluid and evolve with life. You become less attached to the outer forms of purpose, as you know purpose presents itself in every moment.

When you connect to the love that you are and allow your spirit to guide you, you express and engage exactly how and where you need to be for the greater good of all.

You live in sacred alignment rather than external seeking. You know that you are enough. There is nothing to prove. Nothing to become. Life gets to be a dance, full of presence, as you live from your true sense of purpose.

When we are connected to our essence, we are able to hear our intuition, our inner divine guidance, so that we can take action from there, rather than listening and acting based on external voices and expectations.

We are able to stay on course for any intentions our soul desires to experience while we are here, in this physical body.

We are able to know when we are making choices based on love or fear. Are we making decisions based on inner intuition or external expectation? Are we taking aligned and inspired action? Or, are we forcing action based on outside beliefs?

So, how do we connect and embody our true purpose, our soul essence? I will share what works for me and some examples. I invite you to feel within to find what is right for you.

I find my personal connection by disconnecting from all the noise and becoming still. I do this through meditation, prayer, time in nature... taking time and sacred space to feel within, to feel God, to feel a part of something greater, to feel the truth.

EMBODYING ESSENCE EXERCISES

Meditation

Get into a comfortable position, somewhere you won't be distracted or interrupted. Take a moment and feel your breath... feeling the gentle inhale and exhale. No need to adjust it, allow it to be natural. Feel the breath flowing throughout your body, noticing the gentle rise and fall of your belly and chest, the air flowing in and out of your nose, feeling and becoming aware of your entire body as you breathe.

Next, bring your awareness to your heartbeat. Notice the beating of your heart. You may place your hand upon your heart. Feel the beating. Begin to become aware of your beating heart and your entire body, feeling your heart beating life throughout your entire being.

Bring your attention to both your breath and your heartbeat within your body. Notice how they function and sustain you without needing your awareness; they carry on as you carry on...

Allow yourself to connect to that deeper part of you... the soul... the spirit... the God of your understanding... the life force that beats your heart and guides your lungs to breathe...

Feel yourself held in this sacred love... feel yourself connected to the sacred love... feel your oneness to this sacred love...

As you feel ready, gently bring your attention back to this moment, carrying with you the awareness of your deep sacred connection, and essence of love... beyond all that is.

Nature

Find a place that calls to you in nature—perhaps the woods, along the water's shore, in a field, or in your yard. Make yourself comfortable. Relax, and simply witness. The air. The wind. The sunshine. The moonlight. The stars. The birds. The crickets. The sights. The sounds. The smells. Allow yourself to be immersed in nature... allow yourself to feel your connection to nature... the peacefulness... the flow... the rhythm... the beauty... the love.

Prayer

Take a moment and pray how you like to pray. Connect and converse with your Creator. Allow yourself to be open to the conversation.

If you'd like an example to get you started, you may use this and customize to your personal preferences:

Dear God (of your understanding, Divine, Universe, Source...),

I know you have placed me here with purpose. Please help me to feel my true essence, my divine connection, the truth of who I am. I pray for your guidance in helping me to feel and know my purpose. Please illuminate my soul and my essence, so that I may feel within me and know the gift you have placed within my heart, who I truly am, and what I am here for. Please guide me so that I may fulfill my purpose, feel in purpose, and live my true soul purpose.

Thank you. And so it is.

Your essence is your unbounded, pure potential. When you embody your essence, it is the foundation your purpose gets to express and engage through.

WHAT I'VE LEARNED:

When I started my quest for purpose in the second "E" (expression), I turned up empty-handed because I was missing the foundation of me. When I connected to my core energy, my essential essence, my spirit, then the E's that follow (expression and engagement) eased into place.

Your Turn to Reflect.

Use the space below to connect with your essence and share about your experiences from the previous exercises. What essence exercise were you able to connect with the strongest? Did you have any recurring thoughts, feelings or sensations during these exercises?

_____

_____

_____

_____

_____

_____

_____

_____

_____

_____

_____

_____

_____

_____

_____

_____

_____

_____

_____

_____

_____

_____

_____

_____

_____

_____

_____

_____

_____

_____

_____

_____

_____

_____

_____

_____

CHAPTER
Three

*We are all unique expressions
of the same Source.*

EXPRESSING PURPOSE

Love in Action.

*T*he next layer of purpose is expression. This is the layer where most of us start our search, and where we may believe it resides in our doing.

When we start here, it's easy to become lost, as we are starting the search outside ourselves. When we begin inside by embodying our essence, and then build upon that with expression, we can align our doing with our soul.

Expressing our purpose is what we are called to create and to do. This is where we get to tap into our creative potential, our abilities, and our joy.

Expressing is your purpose in action.

You may be saying, "Why can't I simply start here? Why is knowing and embodying my essence so important? Why can't I just get right to the doing?"

First of all, if searching outside ourselves, it's easy to listen outside of ourselves as well. When I started my search with this second E, attempting to answer the question, "What are you going to do with your life?," I followed many "shoulds" to find it.

You should do this. You should do that. Believing that my purpose was my doing and not feeling connected in my essence and its enough-ness, those "shoulds" took me on a journey that didn't fully align, hence the search for "something more."

It is inherent to connect to our inner world so as to not lose ourselves in the outer world.

See, I wasn't listening to my inner callings, I was abiding by outer suggestions and seeking my purpose solely in the form of a career.

When we listen to outer influence versus inner knowing, we can take action based on fitting in, pleasing, expectations, or believing the stories of "I'm too *this or that* to do what I feel called to."

When we are in inner alignment, our outer expression becomes aligned as well. When we are connected and embodied in our essence, we are divinely guided to each action. All is revealed as we move through life with presence.

When you start by connecting to the love that you are, you get to ask and discover, "How does love want to express *through* you?" which makes it a more joyful and fulfilling experience.

Secondly, our expression evolves and changes, which is a wonderful thing! Many times when this happens, if someone solely identifies their purpose with their doing and that doing ceases, so does their perceived purpose.

Say you believe your purpose is raising your children. Once they have grown and left the nest, you may feel a void... "Now what?"

Perhaps you feel your purpose is running a business. If it should no longer be for some reason, you may feel lost... "Now what?"

When we place our sole purpose on something outside of ourselves, and that something shifts in any way, we can feel confused as to who we are and what to do next.

When we start with embodying our essence, and the expression shifts, the foundation is solid and you can rebuild and recreate. It doesn't shake you as much because you know your true purpose cannot be taken away. Instead of "Now what?," it can be an exciting, "What's next?"

Rather than stating, "My purpose is this job," it would be, "I'm currently expressing my purpose through this work."

Essence is the base of your expression. That stays consistent. The forms of expression shift. Love remains, but the expression of love takes many forms. When you are centered in your enoughness and your essence, your expression gets the freedom to play. Your purpose is you, and you get to express yourself in the ways that call to your soul.

We are each unique individuals who possess the ability to sacredly align our expression.

One tool I love to use to sacredly align my expression is being aware of my core values. Core values are like your personal inner compass. They are words that highlight your desired way of living and expressing yourself.

For example, some of my core values are expression, connection, integrity and freedom. When I was feeling out of purpose, I wasn't living according to my values. There were jobs I did where I didn't get to be creative or express myself, or relationships where I felt I couldn't fully express myself for fear of rejection. When I'm not expressing myself, I cannot fully connect. When I'm not being true to who I am, I am not living in integrity. When all of these things are missing, I am anything but free.

Therefore, all the jobs I would try, credentials I would earn, things I would consume, and relationships I would have could never fulfill my purpose because I was not *in* purpose. I was not fully me. I was unaware of my true soul-essence, and I was doing what I thought I "should."

That's the importance of starting with embodying your essence and sacredly aligning your expression—soul-led dreams and living versus society-led searching and succumbing.

You know the love that you are. You are aware of your intuition's guidance and your core values. You build a solid inner connection, so the outer reflection can transform with grace and ease.

Expression takes many forms. It's an opportunity in each and every moment to express the love that you are, in the forms you are called to express.

There is so much potential and possibility within you—so many layers of love to express. When you know your true essence cannot be swept away, it allows your spirit to play in times of change. Feel yourself grounded in you, and there isn't anything you can't do!

JOURNALING EXERCISE

Take a moment and allow yourself to write whatever comes to you... free-flowing words... You may choose to ask yourself questions such as:

- What is my purpose?

- What do I love?

- What did I love as a child?

- When am I the happiest?

- What do I value?

- What is important to me?

- What do I feel would make the world a better place?

- What do I believe?

- What lights me up?

Then, simply allow the pen to flow with no judgment.

Reflect back upon your answers. Sum each one up into one or two descriptive words.

For example: If I answered that I love to be with my family, to be in nature, to go to the beach... a word that may sum this up is "connection" (which translates to one of my core values, a compass that guides me and my desired expression).

WHAT I'VE LEARNED:

While expression is essential, starting here can have us swirling around what we authentically are called to. By coming home to the self first (our essence) and knowing that you are enough simply being, expression becomes an ongoing opportunity to express you... no boxes, no "shoulds"... purely you and what is calling you, in this moment, to express.

Your Turn to Reflect.

You may use this space to answer the journal prompts. As you reflect on these, feel into how they align with your values.

_____

_____

_____

_____

_____

_____

_____

_____

_____

_____

_____

_____

_____

_____

_____

_____

_____

_____

_____

_____

_____

_____

_____

_____

_____

_____

_____

_____

_____

_____

_____

_____

_____

_____

_____

_____

_____

_____

_____

_____

_____

CHAPTER

Four

When doing comes from your being,
all are truly served.

ENGAGING PURPOSE

Love in Service.

*E*ngagement is what enhances the depth of meaning in our life experience. It is the sacred gift of sharing ourselves and this life together.

We are all part of the web of life, and interacting and engaging offers us a feeling of purpose. It's where we get to share the love that we are to create impact and add value. It's how we contribute to society.

Engaging is your purpose in service.

This can be through your work, your offers, your smile, your energy, your prayers, volunteering, spending time together... from the biggest and grandest of things, to the smallest gestures. They all create big impacts—in the world around us and in our feeling of purpose.

Have you ever felt down, but then had the opportunity to help someone in some way, and that lifted your spirits? Or perhaps you were the recipient. That is the power of engaging. Even a simple smile can create a significant impact. We often don't realize the power of our interactions.

Engagement is when we feel that sense of connection, accomplishment, contribution, and adding value. We see, feel, know or believe that we are making a difference in some way.

When you are in your essence, being the love that you are, you can't help but express from there, and when you share that expression, your energy impacts the world. Sometimes it may be in ways that you are not even aware of, but by you simply being present.

That's the beauty of presence and connection within your purpose; you are guided to be exactly where you are to be and when. The opportunity for engaging your purpose is present in each and every moment, you only need to open your eyes and heart to this awareness.

If you are feeling a lack of purpose, ask yourself, "How am I serving? How am I contributing? How can I? How can I share the love that I am in this moment?"

By sharing the love that you are, you are communing with and contributing to life.

Being present on purpose, in your purpose, is where the true magic of life happens. Once I released the need to "arrive" somewhere, and to be fully here now, my life became more joyful and meaningful.

It was no longer about accomplishing my purpose; it became about living *with* purpose by connecting with the love that I am, listening within to how that love wants to be expressed in the moment, and then sharing that love, truly and deeply, with the world.

One day I offered someone a smile and a kind word—seemingly an ordinary thing. I was simply being me. Unknown to me, that was exactly what they needed at that moment. That day, that moment, that smile was my purpose.

If I was too busy thinking about how I was going to fulfill my purpose (somewhere out there) and not being fully present in my purpose (embodied and in the moment), I would have missed the opportunity to engage and express my essence with the very person who needed it in that moment.

You are here to not only be and embrace the love that you are and to express that love in its many forms, but to also share that love... That is the key. Love is meant to be shared. That's how it grows.

The world needs more love. Love is who you are. Love is all there is. Connect to the love that you are, express that love, and share it. The world needs who you are.

SHARE YOUR PASSION

In the first chapter, I mentioned how I wanted "an order of purpose with a side of *passion*."

I remember getting excited as a child, exclaiming that I had found the purpose of life... "Passion!" I saw the excitement and enthusiasm people felt when they were passionate.

"Enthusiasm" actually comes from two Greek words—en: within, and theos: God—therefore, you can say it translates to "God within." When you feel enthusiastic about something, you are fully embodying your essence.

You can also translate passion to *pass-i-on*—in other words, a sharing of yourself.

When we are *in* purpose (embodied in our essence) and *on* purpose (expressing and engaging) we experience passion. When you are expressing and engaging from your essence, you indeed are passing yourself on, sharing your energy, your love and your light.

When you are in this place, you feel lit up! When you are lit up, you are not searching for purpose or meaning. You are being *you* in the moment. You are present. You are fully alive. You are immersed in the energy and the experience.

What are you passionate about? What do you do when time flies? What lights up your soul? How do you follow that passion, that inner fire, that desire? How do you, "pass-I-on?"

Embody the love that you are, express it, and shine your light bright for all to receive the gift of you.

WHAT I'VE LEARNED:

Sharing who we are, our gifts, and our talents is what makes this life meaningful. Our interactions are what add the deepest value. When I connected to myself and honored my expression of writing, the greatest impact and blessing was when I no longer kept those words hidden in my personal notepads, but shared those messages and experiences with others. The magic happens when we share the love that we are, in each and every moment, great and small.

Your Turn to Reflect.

What ways do you engage your purpose? What are some ways you can? How would you love to share your gifts and passion? What creates the feeling of enthusiasm for you? When are the times you've felt this? Ask yourself, "How do I pass-I-on?"

_____

_____

_____

_____

_____

_____

_____

_____

_____

_____

_____

_____

_____

_____

_____

CHAPTER

Five

You came here, simply to love,
with all your being.

LIVING YOUR PURPOSE

Be Love. Express Love. Share Love.

I've found on my journey that searching for your purpose is truly searching for yourself. Yet, once I figured out the answer I was missing, I realized how it eluded me. While I was me in life, I wasn't fully me, hence my search for the missing "more."

I was safely me—the me to get approval, the me to make others happy, the me to fit in, the me to not rock any boats, the me to be a good girl and follow the rules, meet the status quo, listen to all the outside voices and swallow my very own.

If your true purpose is who you are, and you are not fully being you, shining your unique light, you will continue the quest to find purpose (namely, you).

Your purpose is not something that waits for you to get a degree, to write a book, to create a business, to get married and have kids... Your purpose is happening in each and every moment. Your purpose doesn't pause until you "get there," wherever that "there" is for you.

You are living your purpose from the very moment you come into this world. It is simply this "world" that has us forget that simple truth, as it bombards us with the questions, the expectations, the pressures... "What are you going to *do* with your life?"

If we are not honoring who we truly are, our soul purpose, the love that we are, it will show up in our life. It can take on the forms of stress, unhappiness (such as this searching for purpose and meaning), and even dis-ease. Our bodies guide us and let us know when we have steered away from our truth.

When we place pressure on "figuring out" what our purpose is, we miss out on the moment it is living through us... as it is us. We miss heartfelt connections and deeper experiences. We miss out on the depth of life.

This is why it's important to start with essence and embodying, to come back to your heart, your breath, your being, and ground yourself in this foundation of love.

If we seek outside of that space first and focus on the outer, we miss the present moment, the gift to share our purpose. When embodied in our essence and expressing each moment, we can engage where we are called, in this moment—the only moment there is.

We aren't guaranteed to finish the book, to hold the grand babies, to walk down the aisle, to buy the beach house... When we place so much pressure on purpose being a destination to reach or something to accomplish rather than the journey itself, we miss out on the fullness of the present moment experience.

A great way to stay present is by bringing the three E's into each moment: embody, express, and engage.

Pause and ask yourself:

How can I connect to the love that I am? How can I express the love that I am? How can I engage and share the love that I am? Bring you, your divine essence of love, more deeply, presently, and intentionally into each and every moment.

Embody your essence. Be purpose-full—full of purpose, pure potential, and guided by your soul.

There are many expressions of purpose. Choose your purpose-full expressions, aligned with your soul. You are not the roles you play, you are the essence. Life changes and evolves as do we.

There are many opportunities to engage in each moment, stay present and purpose-full, and allow yourself to be divinely guided.

To help stay grounded and centered in purpose, I find a daily ritual or routine keeps me feeling connected. This way, we can anchor in our purpose so that the waves of life don't knock us down as easily.

For me, that looks like starting my day with connection, gratitude and intention. Upon awakening, before my feet even hit the floor, I connect to my breath, my heartbeat, and my essence. I give thanks for the blessing and opportunity of another day. I pray for guidance. I then clarify my personal intention for that day—how is it that I want to feel? And what can I do to create that feeling?

This creates a spiritual connection and a personal embodiment of empowerment before I interact with the outside world. It is a sacred connection to true purpose, before external expectations make their appearance.

If you've been searching for your purpose in all the wrong places, be gentle with yourself. It's normal. It's natural. You are exactly where you are to be, at exactly the right time. The journey you've been on has bestowed many gifts that enhance your expression of purpose.

Purpose has been with you all the while. You're living it. Maybe it's not how you thought it "should" or would look, but it is exactly how you were meant to. Now, you get to do it consciously and feel the depth of the experience, the joy and the alignment!

Life is a messy journey. A brief journey. A blessed journey. You have always been in your essence, now you simply have the opportunity to know it and illuminate it in all facets of your life.

"So, what are you going to do with your life?"

The answer? "Live it." Wherever this brief and winding journey takes you. Live it as *you*. Connect to your essence, embody your expression, share your light... because the world needs who you are, just how you are, right where you are. You are enough.

Connect to the love that is you, and purpose is all you can be and do.

WHAT I'VE LEARNED:

My purpose was always with me. I just couldn't see it or find it because I was looking everywhere else. I believed I needed to become something or do something profound. I thought it needed to be big and evident. Turns out, it's quite simple and epically beautiful. Now, I get to remind myself of this simple truth each day, as the world greets me with expectations to be something more. I am enough. I have enough. And from this place, I get to play. Life becomes fun because "purpose" is who I am. There's nothing I need to become. I already am—as are you.

Your Turn to Reflect.

If you are craving more meaning in your life, what creates meaning for you? How can you create this opportunity and contribute in this way? Is it a feeling you are seeking? How can you create that feeling? We are made in the likeness of our Creator. We are creative beings. You are capable of creating the experiences you desire. Listen within. Be creative. Be curious. Be empowered. Be you.

_____

_____

_____

_____

_____

_____

_____

_____

_____

_____

_____

_____

_____

_____

_____

_____

_____

_____

_____

_____

_____

_____

_____

_____

_____

_____

_____

_____

_____

_____

_____

_____

_____

_____

_____

_____

_____

_____

_____

_____

_____

_____

_____

_____

_____

_____

_____

_____

_____

_____

_____

_____

_____

_____

_____

_____

_____

_____

CHAPTER
Six

*I tried so hard to complicate joy,
while it simply sat in my heart,
patiently awaiting my arrival.*

REALIGNING WITH PURPOSE

Return to Love.

*W*e put a lot of pressure on "purpose." So much so, that if we feel we don't know it, or aren't living in it, our life can feel as if it's missing some value and meaning.

I've felt this many times and can even feel it at times while knowing what my true purpose is. I'm sharing this with you so that you can navigate your journey and be gentle with yourself.

Personally, I believe it's due to the external pressures we've created with it—"What are you here to do?" Or, it can be from trying to measure our purpose or value based on outside standards as well as feeling on a soul-level that something is missing as we go through the day-to-day grind.

I believe it all comes back to connection. To our essence. To our soul. To our spirit. To our Creator. To each other. To our oneness.

As it's been said that we are not humans having spiritual experiences, we are spirits having human experiences—to "be in the world, not of the world..."

For me, these lead to reminding myself to live a soul-led life versus a society-led life. To come back to my essence, to connect to my spirit.. to feel my core, my divine essence of love...That that *is* enough. That I am enough.

Life will offer moments of questioning and feeling lost. This could be through losses, such as the loss of a loved one or a job, or from being criticized or judged—something that will have you pondering it all... Life offers many lessons on "impermanence" that can be challenging to face.

In these moments, we are offered the opportunity to surrender the struggle and connect back to our truth—the divine love that we are—to know that although everything changes, love always remains. It's not always easy. It requires faith and trust. Will we accept the opportunity for growth or fight it? Will we return to the love that we are?

There will be times you ask, "How can I be a space of love in this moment?" There will be times where you may simply need to be held in that space of love yourself.

It is essential to remember that expression forms shift, change and transform, and that that is a natural part of life. It may not look how you think it will, or how you want it to at times, and those times offer the opportunity to connect even deeper within; They allow the opportunity to reflect upon your core values and to bring those into your current expression, or simply to see how they are already there.

Engagement opportunities are always available. All you need to do is be in your heart, be true, see others as hearts and souls before you, and know that simply being you is enough to make an impact.

You are your purpose. You are in it. You are living it. It's merely a matter of coming home to yourself to truly see and feel that and to illuminate it even more as you embody this truth.

You are enough. You are more than enough—right now, in this moment, exactly how you are.

If you find times where you are missing that feeling of purpose and meaning, I invite you to check your "E-Meter."

First, check in with Embodying.

Do I feel I am connected to my core essence? Do I feel the love, light and enough-ness that I am? Connect within; feel your true essence.

Second, check in with Expression.

Do I feel I am expressing the love that I am, in alignment with my core values? Or, am I acting from a place of "should" and expectation? Am I acting from love or fear? Revisit your values. How are you expressing them? How can you?

Third, check in with Engagement.

Do I feel I am contributing by expressing my true essence? Am I shining and sharing my light, or am I hiding and playing small?

How am I measuring my impact? Based on my inner truth? Or the outer world? How am I interacting, contributing and impacting?

The key when checking in is to notice when you hear a judgment from outside yourself. For instance, many times I can feel I'm lacking "engagement" because I'm not creating enough income or serving enough clients, by outside standards, which in turn can trigger that "not enough" feeling.

Engagement is not about income or numbers. Neither is your purpose.

The key is to come back home to yourself and realize that you are enough. Then, remind yourself to not measure yourself by society standards, but to allow your soul standards to guide you. The opportunities to create engagement in alignment with you will unfold in turn.

When I came back to the truth of engaging, I offered myself the questions, "How am I already engaging? And in what ways can I?" My intention came back to that of connecting, adding value, honoring my values, embracing my enough-ness and releasing the need for external validation.

When we come back to the inner connection, we can create external results. If we focus on the external standards to create the external results, we can struggle more and miss the experience of true purpose and joy.

What I've found in times like these is that it's important to pause, reflect and reconnect, for your spirit knows the way that is right for you. Come home to the love that you are, and allow that to be your guide.

You are here to be you, the love that you are, and to grow and expand that love through your unique expression and engagement.

You are a channel of love. Connect to that love. Embody that love. Express the love that you are how it wants to express in this moment. Engage with the world by sharing the love that is you.

Center in the love that you are. Purpose is all that you can be and all that you can do, for purpose is you.

Remember, you are love, and you are loved.

WHAT I'VE LEARNED:

Really paying attention to how you are measuring what you are feeling is so important. There are many times I catch myself basing it on outside standards, and when that is the case, it throws me off my alignment as I am back to searching outside myself and trying to prove. Always come back to essence, enough-ness, and the divine love that you are.

Your Turn to Reflect.

How are you committed to staying connected to your core? Have you checked in with your E-meter? Share what you've found below.

_____

_____

_____

_____

_____

_____

_____

_____

_____

_____

_____

_____

_____

_____

_____

_____

_____

_____

_____

_____

_____

_____

_____

_____

_____

_____

_____

_____

_____

_____

_____

_____

_____

_____

_____

_____

_____

_____

_____

_____

_____

_____

_____

_____

_____

_____

_____

_____

_____

_____

_____

_____

_____

_____

_____

_____

_____

_____

_____

_____

_____

_____

_____

_____

I've let go of trying and finding and figuring out. Now, I relax into love—what life is truly about. One moment at a time, I allow it to unfold. No contorting, no forcing, no doing what I'm told. My spirit knows, my soul guides, the truth of me no longer hides. I embody my essence, express my heart, engage with life—the oneness of which we're all a part.

ABOUT THE AUTHOR

Love, Bobbie Jo is a Certified BodyMind Coach, Author of I Just Want To Be Me and Claim Your Stage, Meditation Guide and Transformational Speaker. She holds a bachelor's degree in communications and business, and previously taught at the university level.

Bobbie Jo believes that the world needs who YOU are.

After decades of losing herself in all life's "shoulds" and expectations, Bobbie Jo reconnected to her personal truth, tossed the societal script, owned her voice and claimed her stage—transforming her life.

Now, she guides others in making the move from stage fright to spotlight, to be all of who they came here to be and to make their impact in the world.

Clients working with Bobbie Jo discover a deeper sense of connection, clarity of personal purpose, confidence in self-expression and the courage to take the steps to create the life and business they truly desire.

To discover more about Bobbie Jo, visit:

lovebobbiejo.com